Super Minds
People With Amazing Mind Power

ACKNOWLEDGMENTS

Animal Children: Information was taken and quoted from the *Daily Star* (London) of April 17, 1991. The feature on Djuma was written by Dennis Newson.

Padre Pio: Information taken from *Padre Pio–The Pierced Priest*, by Jim Gallagher (London: HarperCollins, 1995).

Helen Keller: I am indebted to the summary of Helen Keller's life that appears in *ABC's of the Human Mind* (Pleasantville, N.Y.: Reader's Digest General Books).

Edgar Cayce: All information is from Thomas Sugrue, *There Is a River* (A.R.E. Press).

Hadad the Yogi: Information was taken from Donald Powell Wilson, *My Six Convicts* (London: Hamish Hamilton, 1951).

John Hodgson: With thanks for reading through the book and helping with readability.

Super Minds
People With Amazing Mind Power

Tony Crisp
Illustrated by
Mary Kuper

ELEMENT
CHILDREN'S BOOKS

SHAFTESBURY, DORSET · BOSTON, MASSACHUSETTS · MELBOURNE, VICTORIA

For Hyone

© Element Children's Books 1999
Text © Tony Crisp 1999
Illustrations © Mary Kuper 1999

First published in Great Britain in 1999 by
Element Children's Books
Shaftesbury, Dorset SP7 8BP

Published in the USA in 1999 by
Element Books, Inc.
160 North Washington Street,
Boston MA 02114

Published in Australia in 1999 by
Element Books and distributed by
Penguin Australia Limited,
487 Maroondah Highway, Ringwood,
Victoria 3134

Cover design by Design Section
Typeset by Dorchester Typesetting Group Ltd.
Printed and bound in Great Britain by Biddles Ltd,
Guildford and King's Lynn
British Library Cataloguing in Publication data available.
Library of Congress Cataloging in Publication data available.

ISBN 1 901881 03 2

Contents

Chapter One

The Weird and Wonderful Mind

What would you do if you had a blob of squiggly jelly in a round container about the size of a soccer ball? You could of course scare your friends with it by getting them to touch the wet, slimy jelly. But suppose the jelly talked to you? Suppose it created full-surround virtual reality worlds you could explore? What if it did your homework for you, designed a supersonic plane, or cried—what would you do with it then?

Your brain, sitting inside your head, is just such a pearly-white jellylike substance. It appears quite small if you look at it. But it is the visible body of your mind, and if you explore it in the right way, it is bigger than all the stars and all the planets in the universe. A healthy brain has about ten billion working nerve cells. Because each tiny cell can connect with

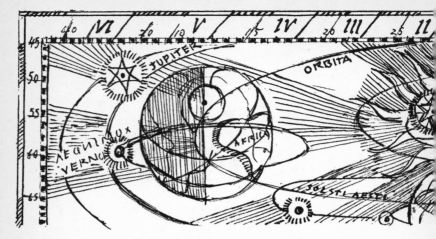

all the other cells, your brain can make more pat-
terned interconnections than there are atoms in the
universe.

The number of these connections is much bigger
than ten billion. In fact, if you wrote the number 1 on
a piece of paper, you would then have to add not just
a few feet of paper to hold all the zeros after the 1,

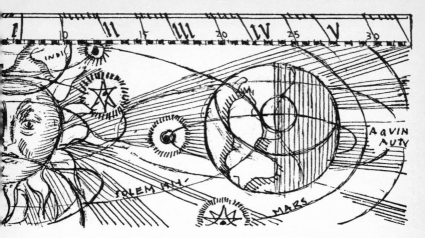

not even a million miles of paper, but about six million miles of zeros! That means your brain can do a lot more than you usually ask it to do!

The Potato You Ate Yesterday Remembers Your Address Today

We often take for granted some of the most astounding

facts about our everyday life. They seem so ordinary that we barely notice them. But just think—the potatoes or rice you ate yesterday can sit and laugh at a TV show today. When you digested the food you ate, in some way that is truly astounding it transformed into your movements, your feelings, your ability to do math problems and enjoy a video. Not even the brainiest person in the world has been able to make a robot that can eat potatoes and transform them into the ability to read this book. If we can already accomplish that amazing feat, what else might we be able to do?

Little Brain—Huge Mind

Your experience of remembering things, laughing, enjoying television, and knowing who you are is called your mind. And we are about to explore your amazing, unbelievable, wonderful mind. We are going to explore the lives of people who do things with their minds that some people do not believe possible.

Solomon Shereshevskii, for instance, remembered everything that ever happened to him and everything he had ever seen—even the license plate number on a car that passed him on the road twenty years earlier. Yes, it's true!

Djuma's parents were killed when he was a baby, and he was reared by wolves in Russia. What do you think his mind was like?

Those are the easy ones. Eileen Garrett was able to hold an object and look into its past, clearly describing the people who used it, their lives, and their surroundings.

Edgar Cayce could apparently look into another person's body, even when the other person was very far away.

Hadad could cure people of serious illnesses, even when they were not present.

You Have an Amazing Mind Too

Even though you're a lot like other people in many ways—for example, you probably have two arms, two legs, two eyes, and so on—some things about you are completely different. You are unique. Not only is your body slightly different in such features as your fingerprints, but your mind is also different and special. There are probably things some of your friends can do that you can't, just as you have skills and abilities they don't.

To explore some of your special abilities, we will try out some of the secret methods people with amazing

11

minds have used to refine their unusual gifts. We will learn how to remember things easily; how to quiet the body and melt fears; how to move beyond our eyes and ears to sense things; how to let our body tell us what it knows; how our body can heal itself; and many more intriguing and remarkable skills.

Get Ready for a Journey into the Mind

Prepare to meet some really interesting people. They will help you discover something of the miracle it is to be you, and some of the amazing things you are capable of. These people's achievements challenge some of the ideas many of us have about what the human mind is capable of, and what the limits of human ability are. These lives suggest that we are much more wonderful than we may think, and that we are part of a limitless and eternal existence.

Chapter Two

The Man Who Remembered Everything

Solomon Shereshevskii's memory was so extraordinary that he could recall every minute of his life in graphic detail. Besides having this remarkable memory, Solomon could "feel" images, "taste" colors, and "smell" sounds.

Solomon was born in Russia about 1886. His talent for remembering things was discovered in 1905, when he was working as a newspaper journalist in Moscow. His editor noticed that Solomon never took any notes at the meetings where each day's work was planned. This irritated the editor enough for him to eventually confront Solomon and criticize him for not doing his job properly.

Solomon was a somewhat shy and awkward person, and the editor's criticism embarrassed him. But when he was questioned, he explained to his editor that he didn't understand why anyone needed to take notes. He asked what purpose they had.

This led the editor to ask more questions and he discovered that Solomon remembered everything his editor had said to him at every meeting. Realizing what an unusual mind Solomon possessed, the editor introduced him to Professor Luria.

A Remarkable Mental Athlete

Professor Aleksander Luria was a famous doctor who helped people with brain damage. He also studied people like Solomon, who had special abilities. Luria immediately wanted to try a series of tests on Solomon. So together they began to explore the limits of what he could remember.

To begin with, Luria asked Solomon to listen to lists of numbers being read out and then repeat them from memory. Solomon was able to recall perfectly the numbers in each of these tests. So Luria gradually increased the length and complexity of the lists, until they contained seventy numbers. Each time, to Luria's increasing astonishment, Solomon was able to repeat the numbers perfectly. If you think of Solomon as a sort of mental athlete, these tests were not even getting him out of breath. In fact, to show Luria a little bit more of what he could do, he repeated the lists backward—without having to hear them again. The tests proved that Solomon's ability to remember was almost boundless. Not only did there seem to be no limit to what he could recall, but each memory was permanent. So fifteen years later, when Luria asked Solomon if he could repeat the lists of numbers without hearing them again, Solomon remembered them all without any hesitation. As before, he could repeat them forward and backward.

Because Professor Luria was a scientist, he wanted to make sure Solomon wasn't faking, and he wanted to find out how such a phenomenal memory worked. He also wanted to know the effects of such a memory on Solomon himself. What was it like not to be able to forget anything—not even the tiniest details of a room you once visited, or the most insignificant feature of a person you once met? So when Luria was convinced that Solomon's ability was genuine, he started to find out just what Solomon could remember.

Imagine having a memory so incredibly sharp that late in life you can still clearly recall your mother's face coming into focus as she bent over your crib. What would it be like to remember every event of your babyhood and early school years? Most adults have forgotten their childhood. In some ways this is a blessing, but it means they can't remember what it was like to feel helpless, or to depend on someone else to do everything for them. Solomon clearly remembered not only what happened when he was an infant, but also what he felt in response to everything that took place.

Your Voice Tastes Good and Seeing You Is Like Musk

Luria discovered that when Solomon experienced something, he didn't simply hear a sound or see something. Instead, his impressions of things seemed to merge together. This means that when Solomon heard something, he might also feel as if he was tasting it; or when he saw something he might also experience it as sound or smell. This ability was not unique to Solomon, and is called "synesthesia."

This blending of all his sense impressions is a clue to Solomon's remarkable memory. When Solomon heard someone speak, the person's voice might sound "crumbly and yellow" to him. Another person's voice was like "a flame with fibers protruding from it." In his book about Solomon, *The Mind of a Mnemonist,* Luria wrote about a time that Solomon refused to buy ice cream from a woman because he experienced her voice as "black cinders bursting out of her mouth."

It wasn't only people's voices that produced accompanying images or sensations. The sounds of words also linked with particular inner experiences. This would often create difficulties for Solomon, similar to the problem he had with the ice cream seller. For example, in Russian the word for "pig" is *svinya*. This sounded "fine and elegant" to Solomon, so it was unsuitable for a pig! The word *khazzer*, however—Yiddish for "pig"—sounded and felt just right to Solomon. It gave him an impression of a pig's "fat

17

greasy belly caked with mud."

These strong mental pictures and sensations were the secret of Solomon's inexhaustible memory. Remembering the long sequences of numbers in Luria's tests had been easy. In Solomon's mind, each number was connected with a particular mixture, a sort of mental hologram or multidimensional experience. These mental holograms were made up of sound, color, taste, touch, and smell. Because each one was different and linked with so many sensory experiences, it was easily memorable. As the numbers were read out, Solomon imagined placing these multidimensional pictures along a road. To remember the sequence he simply imagined walking along the road again, and he repeated the numbers as he "saw" them.

If Only I Could Forget!

For most of us, our memories of experiences fade fairly quickly. But because the multifaceted mental holograms accompanying each experience were so intense for Solomon, he did not lose them as most of us do. The images and impressions would last for hours, crowding his mind and making it difficult for him to pay attention to what was happening in the present.

This was such a problem that Solomon tried various methods to get rid of some of his memories. He tried imagining a great sheet of canvas covering them. He tried writing down the things he wanted to forget and burning the paper. Nothing worked.

Another problem Solomon faced was that he often found it difficult to recognize people he had known for some time, or recognize voices on the telephone. Solomon's awareness of detail was so acute that the slightest change in a person's facial coloring or voice made it difficult for him to recognize them. Most of us would not even notice such small changes of complexion or sound.

A Mental Giant with Problems

Perhaps because of Solomon's difficulty in dealing with the immense flood of impressions he met each day, he did not appear to be a mental giant. In fact, he struggled with things that many of us deal with easily, and in this sense was mentally crippled by his abilities.

Sometimes he was timid and cautious. To many people he looked awkward and mentally slow, spending a lot of time daydreaming amid his vast internal virtual-reality world. He worked at dozens of different jobs trying to find something he could feel skilled at and at the same time use his remarkable abilities. Eventually he worked on stage as a memory man, "Mnemonist," displaying his mental abilities to paying audiences.

The Magic of Imagination

Because of the way his mind functioned, Solomon had other remarkable talents besides memorizing. Being able to walk around his memories and knowledge as if they were a real landscape enabled him to

solve problems that required detailed thought, planning, and visualization.

Solomon also said that he could use his vivid mental imagery to rid himself of pain. He would create an image of the pain, then slowly move that image farther and farther away, until it disappeared over the horizon. At this point, he said, the physical pain disappeared. He could also use this image-making ability to change his temperature. If he wanted to feel warmer he would imagine himself in a hot place. If he wanted to feel cool, he would imagine himself amid ice fields.

Solomon always thought that because of his amazing memory he would one day do something great. Instead he spent most of his time daydreaming, exploring the boundless, clear memories he could

relive so vividly.

However, in 1968 A. R. Luria's book about Solomon was published. It has since become recognized as one of the great works of psychological research. So perhaps Solomon did manage to do his "great thing" after all.

Building Your Own Memory Power

Just as athletes learn special techniques to improve their performance, we can each learn simple ways to improve the way our mind works. Memory is one of the easiest mental abilities to improve. Because the brain has almost unlimited connections for storing information, even people with brain damage can learn an incredible amount.

If you had all your memories locked up in a safe,

and to get to any memory you had to dial a long number, such as 5861497300719430476, it would be best to write it down to make sure you remembered it. But if you could open the safe with a picture of a blue horse standing between two trees, with a big white bird sitting on his head like a hat, it would be easier to remember. And that is the most important fact to learn about memory. Using images helps us remember, just as it helped Solomon. So instead of asking your mind to do things the hard way, you can start using an easy way. You'll find you can remember ten times as much as you usually do, and you already know a lot!

The Mat Sat on the Cat

Using unusual images or funny descriptions to remember names and numbers is fairly simple. With a name, for instance, you can make up a picture that is easy to remember. If you meet someone called

Brian Webster, or Shelley Galloway, create pictures or scenes and words that make you laugh, or are strange enough to be memorable.

For Brian Webster, we could change his name to Brain, and make a mental picture of a big brain on his body, sitting in the middle of a huge spider web, waiting to catch someone. Because we actually have a memory on file of his name as Brian Webster, when we think of him with the weird picture, it will be easy to go from "Brain on the Web" to "Brian Webster."

With Shelley Galloway, a seashell might link with Shelley, and a path to a gallows create a link with Galloway.

But those are my images, and it is best to create your own, made up of pictures or objects you link with the name.

A similar technique can be used to remember numbers or dates. You can either make up your own image to link with a number—for instance, 1 = Dad; 2 = Mom; 3 = Mom,

Dad, and you; 4 = a horse with four legs; and so on. Or you can link numbers with words and the pictures associated with them: 1 = sun; 2 = shoe; 3 = tree; 4 = door; 5 = hive; 6 = sticks; 7 = heaven; 8 = gate; 9 = line; 10 = hen. To remember a date like 1899 you could make a picture of a sun walking through a gate dragging two lines.

This method can also be used with things you have to remember for school. Anything is easier to remember if you link it with an image.

When you use pictures to remember something, you must of course run the picture through your mind several times to record it in memory. You then need to recall it the next day to really etch it into your memory.

The Great Moviemaker

Static images are fine for remembering single facts like names and dates. But for something more complex, like a historical event, or a task you've been asked to do, you need to make a mental movie. It's easier to remember a scene in a film than a paragraph in a book. So make a mental movie of what you are trying to remember. If it's something you've been asked to do, make a mental movie of yourself doing it—and make sure you show yourself having fun while you're doing it. If you don't, you may be subconsciously telling yourself to forget it because you won't enjoy it!

There are lots of things you already have in your memory that are really useful, but not linked to any easily recalled picture or mental movie. These are the things that can be so useful when you're writing an essay or being creative.

At times you might feel you don't know much about a particular subject. For example, if I asked you what you know about trains, you might come up with just a few facts. But try using this clever memory technique: Write the word *train* in the middle of a blank sheet of paper, then write down anything having to do with trains that comes to mind, no matter how crazy or trivial it seems. You'll probably come up with a massive amount of information. At first you might write *tracks*, then *doors,* then *driver,* then *station*—and the words would go on and on, because you know a lot more than you realize. Once you'd written out your words connected with *train,* you could then easily write something about trains, especially if you wrote about your feelings about trains, and memories of train rides.

Your mind is a wonderful treasure house filled with feelings, knowledge, and creative connections. Learn to go in and find those treasures and use them, and you can have more fun than ever.

Chapter Three

Edgar Cayce and the Cosmic Mind

Edgar Cayce had many strange abilities. One was discovered when he was a young child and couldn't remember how to spell the words he was learning at school. After struggling to memorize the spelling words with his father's help, he said, "Daddy, please let me sleep. I'm so tired."

By chance the book Edgar had been learning from was under his head as he slept. When he woke up and his father continued with the lesson, they found that Edgar knew how to spell every word perfectly. In some way his mind had looked into the book as he slept and photographed each word.

When Edgar knew what his sleeping mind could do, he used its abilities to learn all his school lessons. He found it easy, when asked, to stand up and recite a long, famous political speech!

Like some other children, Edgar also claimed to see people who were not visible to adults. Psychologists often explain this as an "imaginary playmate," but Edgar claimed that one of these people was his dead grandfather.

Another unusual ability appeared when Edgar was accidentally hit on the head by a baseball. Just before losing consciousness, he described a poultice that should be put on his head. The poultice was made and applied, and helped Edgar's recovery.

Not realizing just how extraordinary Edgar's abilities were, his parents never mentioned them to people outside the family, in case they thought Edgar was mentally peculiar.

Seeing Beyond the Eyes

When he grew up, Edgar consciously used his abilities to help people. For instance, he was able to prescribe remedies to cure people's illnesses. He discovered this ability when he lost his voice because of stress. In his attempts to find a cure, he consulted a hypnotist named Hart. Hart failed to put Edgar into a hypnotic sleep, but Edgar knew he could do this himself. Working with another hypnotist named Layne, Edgar put himself into a sleeping state. In this state, he looked into his own body and described what needed to be done: he said the hypnotist should suggest to him that the circulation to his throat should increase. This was done, and his throat became scarlet with blood. Gradually the blood flow decreased to normal, and Edgar was told to wake. His voice was restored.

When local doctors heard about Edgar's ability, they started asking him to help them with difficult cases. Gradually his fame spread. In August 1902, Edgar was called to the home of Mr. and Mrs. Dietrich of Hopkinsville, Kentucky. Their five-year-old daughter Aime had been ill for three years. After an attack of flu at the age of two, she had stopped developing mentally and was experiencing up to twenty seizures a day.

The Dietrichs were fairly wealthy and had tried many specialists, with no success. It must have been desperation that urged them to ask a young, rather shy bookstore clerk to see if he could help their only daughter.

Doctor When Asleep

Cayce explained to the Dietrichs that he wasn't a doctor and knew nothing about medicine, or why their daughter was having seizures. The Dietrichs said they understood this, but urged him to continue. Loosening his shoes and tie, Edgar reclined on their sofa and put himself to sleep. Standing nearby, Layne began to ask him questions about Aime. Still asleep, Edgar answered in a clear voice and in great detail.

When Edgar woke up, Mrs. Dietrich was crying. She said, "You have given us the first hope we have had that Aime can recover."

Edgar's only reply was, "What did I say?"

While he was asleep, Edgar had explained that a few days before catching flu, Aime had slipped and hit the end of her spine. One of her vertebrae had been displaced, and this allowed the flu germs to

29

enter her spine. Osteopathic adjustments to the verte-brae would cure Aime, Edgar said.

Aime had the treatment Edgar recommended, and a few days later she spoke the name of a doll, something she had not done since her first attacks. From then on she rapidly developed into a normal five-year-old.

Some years later, on October 9, 1910, Aime's case was reported in the *New York Times.* The article read, "The medical fraternity of the country is taking a lively interest in the strange power said to be possessed by Edgar Cayce of Hopkinsville, Ky., to diagnose difficult diseases while in a semiconscious state, though he has not the slightest knowledge of medicine when awake."

After this story appeared, people from all over the world began to request Edgar's help. Distance didn't seem to be a problem. Edgar would go into his self-induced sleep state and his wife, Gertrude, would ask him to examine the person who had asked for help, no matter how far away that person was. From his sleep state Edgar would describe in medical terms what was wrong in the person's body and mind, and he would suggest ways they could be healed.

Edgar was a poorly educated man who for many years worked as a photographer. But he became so sought after that an organization was formed to support his work, and a hospital was built in which several doctors worked under Edgar's supervision.

You Have Lived Before

Gradually people began asking the sleeping Edgar questions regarding things other than their health.

This was partly because in some "health readings" he mentioned that the person's present illness or life situation was connected with something that had happened in a previous life. While awake, Edgar did not believe in reincarnation, but his sleeping mind saw it as part of the wider scheme of a person's experience.

One man who sought what were called "life readings"—which meant a description of past lives—was Dave Kahn. From his sleeping state Edgar told Dave that he had been an Irishman, and had worked as an aide to Lord Howe, a famous English soldier. Edgar went on to say that General Somerville of the U.S. Army was in fact the reincarnation of Lord Howe, and if Dave went to him, General Somerville, without knowing why, would take him on as an aide.

Dave Kahn got an introduction to General Somerville, and was taken on as an aide. Because of other past life influences, Dave was also advised to go into the wood and metal business. Needless to say, he took the advice—and became a millionaire as a result.

One night, when Edgar and Gertrude were just going to bed, there was a knock on the front door. Edgar answered the door, and Gertrude heard him talking for about an hour. When he came back to bed, Gertrude asked him who it was. The strange reply was that it had been a friend they had known some time ago, but who was now dead. She had come to Edgar to help her understand her situation.

This was not an unusual event for Edgar. He taught

that we already exist as a spirit before we are born. Then when we die in this life, we are born back into that other life. Just as in this life our body is formed from what we eat, drink, and feel, in the life after death we are formed from all we have experienced, thought, and felt during our physical life.

I Know Nothing Yet I Know Everything

Day after day, Edgar's life demonstrated the extraordinary nature of the human mind. While he was asleep he sometimes spoke foreign languages he had never learned—he could actually hold a conversation with someone seeking a reading. His awareness could reach across space and see a place he had never been. For instance, once in a health reading he suggested a particular medicine called "oil of smoke," but the medicine could not be found in any pharmacy. During another reading Edgar gave the name and address of a pharmacy in Louisville, a great distance away. The pharmacist said he didn't know of the medicine, and he certainly didn't have any. So Edgar took yet another reading and this time described a specific shelf in the store. He said the medicine was old stock that had been pushed to the back. The pharmacist looked where Edgar had suggested, and found the medicine.

Because Edgar's sleeping mind would respond to any question, people wondered how he could gather such an amazing store of information. They asked if they could be trained to do likewise. Edgar's reply was that what we are aware of while awake is only a

tiny part of our total awareness. Parts of our mind that are usually unconscious link us with all other minds, in fact with all of history. So when Edgar put himself to sleep, he was able to touch millions of minds and gather whatever information he needed to answer the questions he'd been asked. He said that we are all capable of this, but many of us find it difficult to become aware of our unconscious knowledge.

From the time the organization formed around Edgar, a secretary typed up each reading he gave while asleep. During his lifetime he dictated fourteen million words in this way. They are all preserved at the Association for Research and Enlightenment (A.R.E.) in Virginia Beach, VA 23451, U.S.A. (e-mail: are@are-cayce.com).

Edgar left us a lot to learn.

Learning from Your Own Cosmic Mind

Edgar Cayce's life demonstrated that the mind is much vaster than we may have thought. Although our own personal memories and skills may be limited to what we have experienced and learned, Edgar showed that if we go beyond the edges of our own mind, if we are open to what is bigger and older than our own mind, it may be possible to know what is happening deep inside another person's body; to see or know what is happening far away; to speak languages we haven't learned; to know the ancient events that helped shape our present life; to experience being part of a cosmic mind.

Of course, most of us cannot get in touch with this cosmic mind as easily as Edgar Cayce could. But he taught that dreams can help us, because during sleep we merge with the cosmic mind. Therefore dreams are sometimes messages from this vast mind, telling us something we need to know about our life or actions. Edgar said that if we try to understand and use what we find in our dreams, the wall between our waking self and cosmic self will get smaller.

Perhaps it is easier to understand what the cosmic mind is if we remember that ants, and especially termites, work together in a tremendously connected way. We sometimes call this way of working "instinct." Termites can build the most amazing structures without drawing plans. No architect has to tell them what to do, no slave driver needs to whip them on. Their actions demonstrate a collective "mind" that is greater than the mind of any individual in the colony. This "mind" weaves individual actions into wonderful group creativity. Edgar Cayce taught that humans also have a part of their mind that, if we listen to it, can help each one of us to live in a way that is more satisfying and in harmony with other people and the processes of life. This part of our mind is similar to the instinctive urges that move the termites. We don't need to carefully think or plan. But we do need to quiet our thinking to be aware of our intuitive impressions.

The Power of Dreams

One way to link with the part of the mind that connects us with others is to use the power of our dreams. Start by writing them down in a dream diary. It is then easy to look back and see if you have ever dreamed about the same things before.

Think of everything in your dreams as magical. Even stones in your dreams are alive in some way and can speak to you. Certainly any animals or people in your dreams have a lot to teach you and can become friends, even if they seem frightening at first.

If you do have a frightening dream, try drawing a picture of the dream or making a model of it. Or think of it as a film script that you can change, and carry the plot on past where it ended. This way you can put the frightening dream creature in a cage, for example, until you have tamed it or made friends with it.

Another way to learn from a dream is to sit quietly while you're awake and imagine yourself back in your dream. Again, you can change the plot if you need to. But you can also imagine yourself inside any of the people or objects in the dream. You are a shape-shifter in your dreams, and can become any of the characters you dream about. That is how you get their power and wisdom. When you are the character, notice how you feel, how you think, and how you respond to things. Don't be afraid to explore. If you need help or encouragement, call on the strong, helpful characters in your dreams. By learning to become the different creatures and people of your dreams, you will grad- ually get in touch with your own inner talents and strengths. This is because each part of a dream is a picture of something alive within your own mind and feelings.

Learning to Listen to Intuition

Our intuitive mind speaks to us in much the same way as our ordinary memories come to us. Most of us, however, have made something like tapes or recordings in our mind. So when we think, or try to get a new idea, we often end up just replaying something we read or heard or felt in the past. Listening is a way of quieting those tapes so something new can come to us.

Having intuitive knowledge means that we know something without someone else telling us or experiencing it through our senses. When Edgar examined someone he'd never met while they were many miles away, he was using intuition.

Edgar had a special ability to express in words what he knew intuitively—that is, without having to learn it or think about it. He "listened" to his intuition by putting himself into a sleeplike state, which was his way of quieting his everyday thoughts and feelings. Our everyday thoughts are like loud music. Our intuitive feelings and knowledge are like a quieter musical instrument— maybe a flute—which is easily drowned out by the loudness of our everyday thinking. So learning to listen to your intuition means learning to quiet your thoughts.

When you can do this, you can experience your intuition in different ways. For example, some people have intuitive impressions in the form of spontaneous pictures, like a daydream. Other people hear it, as if someone were talking to them. Most people, though, experience intuition as what they call "hunches." For instance, when I first read about Edgar Cayce I wanted to do something to help the A.R.E. I wrote to say this, but that didn't seem to be enough. Feelings nagged at me to offer more. At the time I was running a book business in the U.K. So I wrote another letter saying I would be willing to sell their books. In a few days two letters came from the A.R.E. in the U.S. The first one said that they were planning a lecture tour in the U.K. and asked if I knew of a bookseller who would handle their books. The second letter said, "The books are on the way. This is a fine case of telepathy." So my "hunch" or intuition came as nagging feelings, a persistent urge.

If your intuitive mind has something important to communicate, you will soon find ideas and feelings trickling into your mind when you learn to listen by quieting your everyday thoughts.

You can practice listening almost anywhere or at any time. Start by looking around you and realizing that no matter where you live, you depend on people working together to bring you the food you eat, the clothes you wear, the TV you watch. Everything around you is the result of people or things working together. Your life is part of a huge network of connections with other people and with life all around you. Hold this in mind. Then quiet your surface thoughts by becoming aware of how your body feels, and perhaps listen to the sounds around you. Don't concentrate on any particular thing, but see if you can let all the impressions happen at once, and see what feelings or urges arise from this. Remember your connection with everything, and open to it to see if you are missing something, or can learn something. Hold that feeling for a few minutes, then go on with your everyday life.

Chapter Four

Eileen Garrett
—Psychic

Eileen was born in the Irish countryside in 1893. Her parents died when she was young, and she was brought up by an aunt. Eileen loved dogs and horses, but was shy with people. They seemed to be insensitive to what she felt.

Eileen's aunt was a very critical person, and Eileen found that she could completely shut out the sound of her voice. So from an early age she discovered she had abilities most people didn't. She could also touch objects and know their inner feelings and history, and see people and children who were invisible to the adults around her. From the age of four onward she had young playmates that her aunt could not see. Her aunt taunted her by insisting they weren't real, but Eileen's "invisible" playmates seemed as real to her as her aunt did. There was only one difference. When she looked at ordinary people she could see what she called a "nimbus" of light—an aura—surrounding them. When she looked at the children they were all light.

The adults who looked after Eileen punished her for talking about the children, so she learned to become secretive.

Seeing Hidden Worlds

Being so aware of the living feelings in trees and animals, and feeling that adults were always lying to each other and to her, Eileen began to think for herself instead of believing what people told her. She learned to watch and observe, and to learn from experience.

Because the auras surrounding people were so obvious and visible to Eileen, it took her a long time to believe people who said they couldn't see them. These auras, which she called "surrounds," told Eileen a lot about what a person was thinking or feeling, or the state of their health. She said, "For me, the important thing about anyone I met, was to see and feel the quality of these surrounds. By their color and their tone, I knew whether people were sick or well." Some people, she said, were surrounded by a gray mist, which showed how unhappy they were. She could see that animals could sense these surrounds, too. When watching people she saw how the colors in their surrounds changed, showing how thoughts and emotions disturbed them as they talked with each other. She could also see, however, that people weren't aware of what caused these disturbances.

Because she was so sensitive to the inner feelings of others, Eileen sometimes found it painful to be around people. For that reason, school was especially difficult for her. To heal herself from the shock of so much emotion hitting her, she learned to allow her awareness, or as she described it, "a fluid part of myself," to flow out to plants, trees, and the earth, and to feel connected with all living things. She developed this ability to the point where she could extend her awareness to people or objects some distance away and feel as if she were part of them.

Death Is a Doorway to Another Life

This ability to see auras, and to touch people's minds, enabled Eileen to see death as something beautiful.

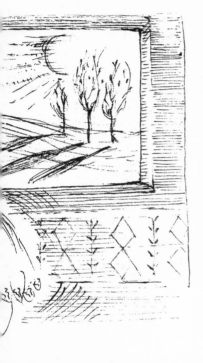

She watched animals and people as they died. The light that had been the person or animal's "surround" left the body at death and started an entirely new life, one not restricted by the body.

When she was a grown woman, Eileen's baby son died in her arms. As he died, she saw the part of him that survived death leave his body. When a person is injured and loses an arm or a leg, they are still very much themselves. Eileen saw that even when her son lost his whole body, there was still a part of him that survived. Even so, the pain of her son's loss made Eileen search more deeply for what happens after death.

She traveled to America to take part in scientific experiments testing telepathy and extension of awareness—what is sometimes called projection, or out-of-body experience (OBE). One experiment took place while she was in New York. One member of the team was in his house in Newfoundland. The test was to see if Eileen could observe what the doctor in Newfoundland was doing and saying while she was still in New York.

Eileen moved her awareness away from her body to the house in Newfoundland, and felt she was actually there. In her own words, "I was able to see the garden and the sea, as well as the house I was supposed to enter; I actually sensed the damp of the atmosphere and saw the flowers growing by the pathway. Then I passed through the walls and I was inside the room in which the experiment was to take place."

With her special abilities, Eileen didn't have to be dead to be a "ghost" and pass through walls.

I Travel Faster Than Light

Once she was in the house, Eileen at first couldn't find the doctor in the room where he should have been. But within moments she saw him walking down the stairs with his head bandaged. As this was happening, she told the researchers in New York what she saw. So she was operating in two places at once. She was able to describe to the team in New York objects the doctor had placed on a table for her, and also repeat words

44

of a book the doctor took from his library shelf and read.

When the results of the experiment were sent to him, the doctor confirmed all of Eileen's observations, and explained that he had injured his head just before the experiment. That was why he had been late entering the room, and why his head was bandaged. By taking part in such scientific experiments, and with the support of people like Edward Carpenter, who had made a study of the extrasensory perception (ESP) she experienced, Eileen gradually developed a view that life is continuous.

45

"Birth and death," she said, are "necessary phases of an eternally changing cycle which strives towards the perfection of man's soul." Just as one day in our life is only a part of a longer, ongoing process from which we learn and grow, so she felt that our whole lifetime is like a day compared with the eternity of which we are a part. We have other "days" in this eternity, from which we will also learn and develop.

Eileen also felt that her supersensory abilities to see beyond what the eyes can see, to hear beyond her physical ears, to move through space faster than her body ever could, were powers that many more people will develop as they open their minds to such possibilities.

Entering the Temple of the Animals

Through watching how plants and animals live, Eileen believed that it is only humans who fear death and make it such an awful thing in imagination. If we could let our instincts or intuitions about life guide us, as animals do, we would be spared a lot of pain and fear.

Eileen said that by living close to animals she learned things about life and death that many people fail to understand. But Eileen didn't simply stand in a field or forest and watch rabbits and squirrels at play. She moved into another dimension of her mind, where she saw beyond what her eyes, ears, and nose told her. Obviously, this isn't easy for most people to do, but it *is* easy to start developing the ability to receive more from the inner life of your mind. One of the simplest ways of doing this is to give your body and feelings the opportunity to express themselves spontaneously.

Most life processes consist of spontaneous movement, which happens without our conscious control, such as our breathing, heartbeat, digestion, sneezing, and yawning. What we often don't realize is that the mind also has ways of communicating spontaneously—one of the main ways is through dreaming.

If we can only learn how to listen, the unconscious wisdom of our being can speak to us. Many ancient cultures understood this, and saw dreaming as a holy experience. In those cultures, a person who couldn't enter into this experience was seen as lacking a normal ability.

The simple activity I am going to describe is aimed at creating the mental and physical readiness to allow your intuitive mind to communicate. If you've never experienced your intuition before, it may at first seem clumsy, like someone who has been tied up for years suddenly trying to move freely. So you will need to practice once or twice a week until it becomes easy. You also need to be ready to let your imagination have some freedom, and not to stop yourself from expressing things because they seem "silly" or "pointless." It's those attitudes that keep us from our inner life. As we've seen, many people judged Eileen Garrett as silly or said she was lying when she gave expression to her intuition. What people did to her, we might be doing to our own intuition.

Being a Seed

To practice this activity you need about twenty minutes to half an hour when you will not be disturbed. You need floor space, preferably on a carpet or blanket, big enough for you to lie full-length on if necessary. It's best to wear fairly loose clothing that allows you to move easily. And it can be very helpful to have a sympathetic friend with you to watch or join in.

When you are ready, stand in the middle of your space. Stand with your feet about shoulder width apart and your arms stretched above your head, making an X shape with your body.

Now close your eyes and hold in your mind the idea of a seed, one that has not yet been planted. It can be any kind of seed you like. Don't struggle with this, just gently think about it.

As you hold the seed in your mind, compare it with the way your body feels. Does the shape of your body feel like a seed right now? For many people, standing with their legs and arms apart *doesn't* feel like an unplanted seed. So, without trying to think about it, but just following how your body feels, try moving your body until you feel more like a seed.

Where Will I Grow from Here?

Learning to follow your body's basic feelings and sensations is important. Let them lead you until you find a position that feels right. As you get to this, ask yourself what a seed feels like before it's planted. It can, after all, remain dry and without apparent life for many years. Is it asleep? Is it waiting patiently? Without trying to be scientific, let yourself have something of the feeling of the unplanted seed.

When you feel ready, shift yourself into being a seed that has been put into warm, moist soil, where it can start to grow. This can be a wonderful experience, and the way to get the most out of it is not to think about how a seed grows, or try to act it out. Just lie in the warm soil and let things happen. If you're not sure how to do that, remember that when you yawn or stretch in the morning, you don't think about it. Your body does the movements automatically. So just keep still until something starts to urge a movement.

Maybe it starts as a little twitch of your head or fingers. Whatever it is, let it happen without trying to direct it or know where it is leading.

I Can Grow Forever

Once your growth starts, let it happen and it will carry through to a point where you will know it is ended. If you have learned to allow spontaneous movement—the kind that happens when you yawn, sneeze, breathe, laugh, or cry—then a most mysterious, wonderful, and surprising emergence of experience and feelings will happen. Because you didn't think it up, whatever comes to you will be new, fresh—and it might even teach you something.

You may need to practice this activity a few times in order to experience it fully. Or you might be lucky the first time and have the wonderful experience of being a seed. Whatever happens, it is worth practicing again and again, because the source of the inspiration that comes seems to always have something new to show you. I have been doing the seed meditation for nearly thirty years, and I still find new treasures every time I do it. You will, too.

Chapter Five

Hadad—
The Rogue Yogi

Dr. Donald Wilson discovered Hadad while he was researching drug addiction in Leavenworth prison in Kansas.[1] Little is known of Hadad except what Dr. Wilson was able to observe in the short time he knew him.

Hadad was a black man, possibly born in Senegal, West Africa, to Senegalese and Hindu parents. His own descriptions of his background were more exotic. Speaking in a wonderful Oxford accent, he described himself as "a Chaldean astrologer with direct line of forebears back to 400 B.C." He also said he had been educated at the universities of Carthage and Oxford, and was a zombie priest from Haiti. He told Dr. Wilson that he had been initiated into secret and ancient blood rites that gave him immense powers.

The facts were that Hadad had been imprisoned on a murder charge. In the 1940s he had been the "hit man"

[1] Donald Powell Wilson, *My Six Convicts* (London: Hamish Hamilton, 1951).

in a terrorizing gang who had been captured when the police, after an impressive car chase, had riddled their car with machine-gun bullets. After the car careened off the road into a cornfield, Hadad was found hiding in the trunk, completely unharmed. This was mysterious, since the rear of the car was full of bullet holes. The only explanation Hadad gave was, "I found it expedient to deflect the bullets from the anatomical headquarters of my spirit."

The meeting between the doctor and the yogi occurred because Hadad was a remarkably skilled escapologist. He had decided that he'd like to see a show, so he escaped from his cell and was later seen by one of the prison staff walking out of a Kansas City theater. His explanation was, "It has been some

time since I have been to a concert, and I felt it would be such a shame not to go. After all, I am just a short distance from the city."

He Died in Solitary Confinement

For his truancy, Hadad was put in solitary confinement for fifteen days. In solitary, Hadad was naked—to reduce risk of suicide, he wasn't even allowed a blanket. He ate only bread and water, had no light, and the guard checked on him through a peephole. When the guard, Thompson, realized that Hadad had not passed any urine for some time, he called Dr. Wilson to check on the prisoner. The doctor and Thompson called to Hadad, but there was no response, so Thompson opened the steel door of the cell. In the glow of his flashlight, they could see Hadad's naked body hanging against the bars of the cell, with a belt around his neck. His apparently lifeless body was cut down, and the belt was identified as belonging to a relief guard, Red.

"What's holding up your trousers these days?" Red was asked. He assured Thompson and Wilson that he was wearing his belt as usual, but when he looked, he found a piece of rope around his waist. Hadad had hypnotized him and convinced him to hand over his belt while believing that he was still wearing it. This frightened Red so much that he asked to be transferred from solitary duties.

A quick examination showed that Hadad appeared dead, even though the belt was not tight enough to have caused strangulation. As usual with a prison death, an autopsy—a thorough medical examination of the corpse—was scheduled to take place three days later. In the meantime, Hadad was placed on ice in the morgue.

It was a Sunday morning when Wilson, with two other doctors, Fellows and Gordon, gathered for the autopsy. It was decided that Fellows would make the first cut, opening the abdomen to extract the heart and lungs. Then the top of the head would be cut open to examine the brain.

Fellows picked up the scalpel to begin, but the three of them suddenly froze as Hadad's corpse rippled into life and took a long, deep breath. Fellows dropped the scalpel as Hadad said, in his perfect Oxford accent, "Gentlemen, I would rather not, if you don't mind."

Cataleptic trance—the appearance of being dead—is not uncommon in medical and occult literature. But being able to come out of such a trance at will, as Hadad had, was, if not unique, extremely unusual. So when Wilson and Gordon next examined Hadad they were curious about how he had done it.

Hadad was ready to explain. He had used his apparent death, he said, to bring his abilities to their attention. But knowing that as doctors they were skeptical, he decided to give them an even more convincing demonstration. He reminded them that in the prison hospital there were a number of epileptic patients who experienced uncontrollable seizures several times a day. At that time, medical science had not yet found a way to stop the seizures—but Hadad said he could, if the doctors would let him try. The doctors agreed.

"I will again enter a three-day death," Hadad told them. "This time I will cause all the seizures to halt for those three days. I will also make the signs of the zodiac appear on my body."

The doctors, knowing Hadad's power as a hypnotist, thought that he might very well have already given the patients a hypnotic command to stop their seizures. But even if this was theoretically possible, no one had ever been able to do such a thing before, certainly not on the scale that Hadad was proposing.

An Unsolved Mystery

For three days the epileptics in the prison stopped having seizures. For three days Hadad once more entered a cataleptic state in which he was apparently dead. For three days the signs of the zodiac appeared on his body in the form of raised welts.

After this amazing display, Hadad offered to pass on his secrets to Wilson and Gordon. They refused. They had many reasons for doing so. Hadad was a murderer, and had admitted to murders even the police hadn't known about. "Having hypnotized us, he could have incapacitated us physically or crippled us neurologically," said Wilson. "He could have left us mentally dissociated. We could have awakened from the trance insane. He could have given us amnesia for our scientific background and training, and left us wild-eyed exponents of the occult. We had no way of knowing what he might do. He might have killed us."

That ended the relationship between Wilson and Hadad, who was reabsorbed into the immense prison system. Hadad's unique abilities and personality must have led him into many other adventures and have left impressions on many other people. But his strange life style kept him out of the public eye, and so a veil hangs over the end of his life.

Yoga Secrets

What were Hadad's secrets? The methods he used to induce his apparent death were connected with the form of yoga breath control called *pranayama*. Training in this form of yoga usually includes strict rules against harming any living creature. The practitioner learns to gradually increase the time between one in-breath and the next. Hadad had learned this skill to an extraordinary degree, where he could hold his breath long enough to appear dead. Sensitive modern instruments have shown that the heart does not actually stop when this happens, but fibrillates or quivers.

Hadad's hypnotic skills also had a long history, as hypnosis has been used for centuries in the East and in many ancient cultures. Yogis use it as a means of self-discipline, and many tribal healers—such as the African *ngaka*, who is often known as a witch doctor, diviner, healer, and herbalist—are masters of hypnosis and suggestion. In these cultures this skill was for centuries a part of communal life, and used effectively for mental and physical healing.

Safe Yoga Skills You Can learn

Pranayama and the skills of the *ngaka* need a lot of training, but there are skills you can teach yourself. Learning to regulate your breath, for example, is a good way of calming your mind and nervous system.

A classic yoga method of breath control uses a 1 - 4 - 2 rhythm. This method is perfectly safe AS LONG AS YOU DO NOT STRAIN BY HOLDING YOUR BREATH FOR TOO LONG. Therefore you need an adult to supervise your first few practice sessions.

Sit comfortably in an upright but relaxed position. Close your eyes and, if you've been moving around, wait for your breathing to level off. Then breathe in

for a count of 4, hold your breath for a count of 16, and breathe out for a count of 8. This is a suggested number that you will probably be able to do, but it is important to find a count that is easy for you to do without straining. So if it is too easy, take the in-breath count higher until you are controlling your breath, but not straining. Keep the 1 - 4 - 2 rhythm. For instance, if you breathe in for a count of 6, you would hold the breath for a count of 24, and breathe out for a count of 12. If the starting count of 4 is too high, drop it down to 3 or 2, adjusting the other breaths as necessary.

Once you find your comfortable count, repeat the whole cycle ten times. As you breathe, notice whether you are tensing your body in any way. If so, drop any unnecessary tensions so you are as relaxed as possible. Remember—no straining. Let your attention rest just on the counting and your physical sensations.

Your breath is constantly mirroring your feelings and mental reactions. Even when you're just reading a story, your breathing and heart rate will change as you imagine various parts of the story. Therefore, by consciously regulating your breath, you can smooth out these mental and emotional waves. Breath regulation is also a great help in dealing with anxious feelings about such things as exams. Even if you don't think you suffer such fears, it is an excellent practice, and if you do it daily for two or three months you'll start to notice how much calmer you are, and how you can slow down your mind and body more easily.

Chapter Six

Schermann— Graphologist Extraordinaire

Graphology, the study of handwriting, has many uses. Some businesses employ graphologists to analyze the handwriting of job candidates. The graphologist can describe the person's strengths, weaknesses, and possibly even special skills. Similarly, individuals may ask a graphologist to help them discover what careers would make the best use of their natural talents. The police use handwriting experts in forgery cases.

One of the greatest modern graphologists was an Austrian by the name of Herr Schermann. From early childhood, Schermann, instead of collecting stamps or coins, was fascinated by envelopes. He amassed a huge collection and would sit looking at the handwriting, trying to form pictures of the people who had written them, and telling himself stories about them.

As Schermann grew, so did his interest in handwriting. Like any graphologist, he studied how people shaped their letters, how heavy the writing was, how deeply it slanted, and so on, but there was also another dimension to his skill. He appeared to "see" the person who had written the words. Some sense beyond those of sight, hearing, smell, taste, and touch was operating. Some intelligence beyond a sharp mind was at work. Because of his skill, Schermann became famous in Austria and worked for the police and other large organizations during the 1920s and 30s.

We Write What We Are

Whether or not we're aware of it, when we write our whole body takes on a certain posture. Our age and state of health affect our movements, too, so they are also evident in the subtle actions of writing. Even our moods and emotions can affect the way we write. Therefore the marks we make on paper are the result of what is going on in our body and mind when we're writing. What Schermann did was to project the process backward, to build up a living impression of all the feelings, the movements, and the type of body and mind that created the writing.

Cornelius Tabori, a journalist who investigated Schermann in Austria, described what happened when he showed the graphologist an envelope written by a woman Schermann had never met. "Schermann looked at it briefly and then started to work. He described the woman's hair color, how she looked, her figure, even her face. Suddenly she seemed to come alive before me in Schermann himself, because he imitated her voice and the body movements she made. To my amazement he told me the story of her life. It was uncanny the way he had become part of her, and told me exactly about settings, people, and objects important to her, even to talks we had shared. I had never experienced anything like it before."

Something that no other graphologist before Schermann had ever managed to do was to be able to look at a person, then reproduce his or her handwriting. This is one of the clues to Schermann's great skill. His insights into handwriting linked it completely with the person and all aspects of their body and mind. Because of this ability, doctors often asked Schermann to diagnose illnesses by looking at a sample of the patient's handwriting.

An Image in the Handwriting

Herr Schermann often worked with the police. One of his most famous cases was a bank forgery. His work on this case went far beyond determining whose handwriting was being examined.

On June 28, 1922, the Wiener Bank received a letter from someone signing himself as Herman

Zagg. In the letter, he said that on June 23, £80,000 had been deposited in his account. He now wanted the Wiener Bank to transfer all the money to another account in a different bank.

The Wiener Bank's ledger was checked, and the entry for the deposit was there. The transfer would have gone ahead if it hadn't been for the carelessness of a junior bank clerk. Instead of entering the transfer right away, he left the pay slip for two days. Therefore, to make sure the money was still in the account, and to avoid being caught for negligence, the clerk went to the carbon copy of the ledger instead of going into the bookkeeping office for the ledger itself. He was amazed to find there was no entry for the account.

Realizing something was very wrong, the clerk immediately reported the matter to his superiors. It was then discovered that someone had written in the £80,000 at the bottom of the day's entries. The writing appeared to be that of the young woman who wrote up the entries, and so she was suspected of forging the entry to get the money.

Someone was immediately sent to the address Herman Zagg had given. No one of that name lived there. Obviously someone within the bank was the forger, and was working with an outside accomplice. The police were called in to investigate, but could not discover who the forger or accomplice were.

The bank then asked Schermann to help. He looked first at the letter the bank had received from Zagg. "The person who wrote this is a tall, fat man," he said. "His work calls for much concentration, has led to eyestrain, and needs little physical activity. Most of the time he is bending over his work. It is not mental work, but he needs to be precise and accurate. He is probably a watchmaker or goldsmith."

From this the bank could assume the writer posing

as Zagg was not a staff member. But whoever made the entry in the bank ledger must have been an employee. So Schermann was asked to look at the handwriting of fifty of the bank's employees.

Among the fifty was a man named L.B., who Schermann said was the forger. It was not the young woman in charge of the ledger. "This man," Schermann said, "is someone who has long planned this crime. He studied the writing of the woman for a long time, and is an artist at copying people's handwriting. He needed an outside accomplice. I have a mental picture of him persuading the goldsmith, promising much gold for him to work with. L.B. knows the forgery has been discovered. Therefore I need a sample of his handwriting today, to see what he is planning."

Genius at Work

Looking at the new sample, Schermann's analysis was that "the man knows he is going to be discovered. Yesterday he explained to his parents that he has committed a crime, and asked them to forgive him. Both parents are ill, and his mother said she would commit suicide if he were sent to prison. It would be difficult for his father to survive also. I can see L.B. is going to say he is innocent until the very end. If you agree not to tell the police I will get him to confess. I want him to remain free to support his parents."

So far, no money had actually been stolen, so the promise was given. The young man was then called to the office and accused of the crime. As Schermann had predicted, he maintained he had nothing whatever to do with the forgery. Then Schermann asked him to write and sign the following:

"Wiener Bank-Verein
Organizations-Bureau
I have nothing to do with the hundred millions.
Vienna 11 July 1922"

Writing these few words betrayed L.B's secret motives. The man's first name was Ludwig, but he had started to sign his name as "Loui(s)." He quickly crossed out this mistake and wrote "Ludwig." Looking at this, Schermann faced him and said he had taken a goldsmith as an accomplice, and that he had told this man his plans to escape to Paris and use the name Louis.

The forger's confidence was shattered, and he

gave a full confession. His accomplice turned out to be a goldsmith who weighed 252 pounds. So Schermann had not only correctly assessed the forger and his motives, but had also given an exact description of the accomplice. The forger also revealed details about his sick parents that agreed with Schermann' s description.

The young forger was dismissed from his job, but no charges were pressed. Because of Schermann's kindness, the man was able to continue his life without a criminal record. He later wrote a letter thanking Schermann for saving him from prison and complete disgrace.

Chapter Seven

Journey through the Mind

Jesse Watkins had led an ordinary but adventurous life until the day when the doors in his mind opened, revealing experiences he had never previously thought possible.

Jesse was born on December 31, 1899. In 1916, when he was nearly seventeen, he went to sea on a tramp steamer and remained on it through the First World War. His first voyage was to northern Russia in very rough seas. During this first year of service, his ship was torpedoed while in the Mediterranean.

Later Jesse worked on a square-rigged sailing ship, and during the Second World War he served in the British Royal Navy as a commander and commodore of coastal convoys. From his earliest years he loved sketching and painting, and late in his life he became a sculptor. But during his years at sea he experienced shipwreck, mutiny, and murder. So he had a varied life, and frequently met danger and the unknown.

The Door in the Mind

When he was thirty-eight Jesse experienced several things that were probably instrumental in opening the doors of his mind. He had moved to different surroundings and changed his way of life. His work was very demanding, and he was working seven days a week, often late into the night.

Jesse was at an emotional low point when something happened that upset him even more. He was bitten by a dog, and the bite would not heal. Eventually he had to go to the hospital to have his wound treated while he was under general anesthesia. That was when his extraordinary journey began.

When Jesse came home from the hospital, things looked different. Time seemed to slow down and gradually go backward, as if he were on some sort of conveyor belt taking him into the past. "This gave me a rather panicky feeling," he said. He felt he wasn't in control of what was happening, and he didn't know where he was being taken.

These feelings changed when Jesse looked in the mirror. He appeared the same but at the same time unfamiliar, and suddenly he felt he was in control of his mind and body in a much more powerful way than ever before.

To Jesse everything seemed clear, because he was experiencing what he was talking about. But when he tried to explain his new feelings to his wife, it sounded to her as if he was just "rambling on." When Jesse began talking about going back in time, glimpsing past lives, and having new abilities, his wife grew frightened. Imagine how you might feel if someone close to you, whom you thought you knew well, suddenly claimed to see and experience things you couldn't see and had never heard anyone talk about. It would probably be quite disturbing.

Jesse's wife sent for the doctor, and Jesse was taken back to the hospital for observation. Jesse says that people "looked at me as if I were mad. I could see the look on their faces. I felt it wouldn't do much good to talk to them because they thought I was round the bend."

Jesse's journey of the mind now took him into even stranger regions. He said that when he got to the hospital, "I felt as if I had died. It seemed to me as if the other people in beds on the ward were all dead too, and waiting to move to the next department of life."

Alive Yet Dead

Traveling into the depths of the mind is not an uncommon experience, and is described even in ancient myths and folklore. To get some insight into what was happening to Jesse, it might help to think of our personality, and our sense of who and where we are, as being like water in a goldfish bowl. The water has a shape determined by the restrictions of the bowl. If it could describe itself, it might say it was round. But if we poured the water into the ocean or a river, it would feel its boundaries melting away, and so it would lose its sense of who, what, and where it was.

Similarly, most people gain their experience of life only through the body's senses, and through the beliefs they are brought up with. Most of us believe we *are* the shape of our body, and we can only do what it can do. However, as we can see from the lives of Jesse and some of the other people described in this book, our mind can sometimes reach far beyond the body's five senses. When we first find the narrow walls of our senses disappearing, most of us feel some panic, and may fear we are dying. That is probably what was happening to Jesse.

Jesse's journey was not over. His feeling of extending backward went further and further, and he became aware of experiencing life as an animal. In fact, he felt he had actually been all sorts of animals, from the lowest life forms up to a human being. So at times he felt like a squirming blob of life without a brain, then like a rhinoceros, and then like a human baby. Jesse felt each experience fully, as we do in a dream that we are totally convinced is real. However, the difference was that Jesse was awake, without the escape hatch of realizing that he was dreaming. There was no "ordinary" world to escape back to.

As disturbing as this condition was to Jesse, he discovered that he had powers in this state that he didn't possess in his ordinary state of mind. When the nurse came to bandage Jesse's wounded finger, he felt that he could now control the way his finger healed. So he told the nurse, "My finger will be okay if you just leave it." He took the bandage off, and gave his finger what he called "intense attention." The next day it was completely healed. He tried giving this "intense attention" to some of the other men in the ward who were agitated, and the men became calm.

I Have Always Existed

Another way of trying to understand what happened to Jesse is to imagine spending your entire life in one small town, then one day going up in a helicopter, high above the town. Suddenly you would be able to see, all at once, every place you had been at different times in your life. And besides all the places you had been, you'd also be able to see places you might not have known about before.

Jesse, in his journey into the mind, said that "I was more than I had ever imagined myself. Not only was I living my life now, but I had existed from the very beginning of time, from the lowest form of life up to the present. The real me was all that experience. Then at times I could see ahead beyond even the awareness I now had, to where we become aware of it all."

Jesse felt that the new "world" he was experiencing was something all humans were moving toward, but most people couldn't reach yet. In that world were beings Jesse called gods, beings who could live and move easily in that world, beings who were not afraid of the enormity of the experience. Jesse felt that everything that happens to us in our life helps us evolve toward becoming like the gods he met.

But the experience was too much for Jesse. "I had suddenly met something so much greater than myself that I couldn't take it," he reported. "So I decided to stop the experience."

Jesse's journey lasted ten days. On the tenth day,

he closed the door in his mind and returned to the world of time and physical limitations.

Learning from Jesse's Journey

The psychiatrist R. D. Laing wrote about Jesse's journey in his book *Politics of Experience.* Jesse and Dr. Laing both believed that Jesse's experience was not madness, but something above or beyond normal experience.

In many older cultures such as the Native American, the Indian, and some African cultures, a person who went on a journey into the mind as Jesse did was treated as a holy person, a priest or priestess. The visions they experienced were valued and seen as useful to the community. The timeless place of mind they managed to reach into was thought of as the real Temple of life, the real place of spiritual wisdom. In these cultures the priest or priestess's work was to go in and out of this Temple, which was not an actual building. It was seen as a place beyond time where one could discover a vast view of life and its meaning. It was a place, or a mental state, such as Jesse experienced. When a priest or priestess reached this state of mind, like Jesse they could direct healing power to others, they could see future events and make prophecies, they could see people's inner qualities and advise them, they could even talk with the dead. For the people in their community, these priests and priestesses were like a window to the world beyond the senses.

Men and women were trained to take on this role,

or supported if they had a gift for it. Jesse had no such training or support. He was thrown into the timeless state of mind as a result of working too hard and having a physical shock. For people such as Jesse, thrown in by shock, illness, or drugs, there is possible danger, just as there is for someone who is suddenly dropped into deep water without knowing how to swim. It doesn't help that in many modern cultures people who have experiences like Jesse's are treated as if they are mentally ill.

Training to Enter the Great Temple

The state of mind in which we stand beyond our small life span in the present life, in which we know we are connected at a deep level with all living things, is not a physical place. If all of us were rivers, the Great Temple (that is, the timeless state of mind) would be the sea we all flow into, where we blend into each other. It is where our individual mind experiences the feeling of merging with all other living things. The Great Temple contains all living things, and has been involved in life from the beginning. To be able to see and enter the Great Temple, there are things we must learn and skills we must develop.

Learning to Look beyond Single Things

Over thousands of years of evolution, humans have had to develop certain skills necessary for survival. One of these is the ability to see dangers or opportunities in the world around us. We see *things*—a person, a book, an animal, or a tree. We use our minds and feelings mostly to determine if the things we see and hear around us are dangerous or helpful. Taking this narrow view of things prevents us from seeing the web of life that we're all part of.

To start seeing like a dweller in the Great Temple, try looking at a tree or animal as a separate thing. Then start to look for ways the tree or animal is connected to everything around it. For instance, what would happen to a tree if there were no air or sun? Take the time to recognize as many such links as you can. If you ever think you've discovered them all, think again—there is depth after depth to find.

When you begin to detect the links of life, go beyond thinking about them and see if you can feel something about them. Then try looking at yourself, your parents, or a newborn baby.

The Great Temple is where we are all linked. To enter it, we must see what connects us all.

Receiving Strength from the Great Temple

When we, or people and animals we love, are troubled or ill, we can gather strength from being able to touch the state of mind beyond human ills and time. As your eyes begin to open through seeing the links you have with the rest of life, you may begin to see how much you are receiving from the process of life and society all the time. This can become a strength you can share with others.

To get strength from the Great Temple, imagine that you are standing in sunlight and letting it go deep into your body. Make no effort, just open up to it.

Then let the pleasure of it flow through you to people you love.

The Secret Key to the Great Temple

If you gradually learn to see that your life depends on the great giving of the sun and earth, and the plants and animals, if you see the links we all have with each other, then it will be obvious that the great key to the Temple is love.

Learning to love is not easy, because we must learn to give of ourselves to care for others. Through love we learn to stand out of the way and let the power greater than our small self live through us. When we learn that type of love, a greater life opens to us, one that is a doorway to a wider life.

Chapter Eight

Padre Pio— Modern Saint

When we look at the things Padre Pio experienced in his life, things seen by witnesses and doctors, we may believe there is no scientific explanation for them. Such things are often called supernatural. The word means beyond the natural, or outside of nature. But "supernatural" is not really an accurate word, since all things are part of the natural universe in which we live. So it would be better to say that what Padre Pio experienced were natural events we do not yet understand, or have not been able to measure or explain.

Padre Pio was born in southern Italy in 1887. He joined the Capuchin Friars, a group of Catholic monks, in 1903, when he was sixteen. At twenty-three he became a priest in the order.

Pio's childhood and adolescence had been unremarkable. He had been healthy and active, working on his father's farm. But in the summer of 1918, when he was thirty-one, something science cannot explain touched his life. He was praying alone in the mountain friary at San Giovanni Rotundo. All was quiet on the mountainside, and there was an intense stillness within the priest, too. So quiet were his mind and feelings that he passed into a state where all thought stopped, yet he was still awake. He lost all sense of time and described his condition as one "similar to sweet sleep." Suddenly the silence seemed to penetrate him, and he saw Christ standing before him, bleeding from his wounds.

Pio was so moved by the vision that he felt as if his chest would burst open. Then, when he came out of the "sweet sleep," he realized that his own hands, feet, and side were bleeding, and showed the same wounds as he had seen on Christ.

A Doorway Beyond Time

From that time on, Padre Pio became a doorway through which powers and attributes from another dimension of life poured into the everyday world.

For instance, Padre Pio appeared to become critically ill at times. Some doctors said he had tuberculosis, at that time a killer disease. Other doctors could find no sign of the disease, but could see his ravaged body. They also witnessed the signs of illness appear and then suddenly disappear.

One day while Padre Pio was in bed struggling to breathe, his face red with fever, Father Paolina of Casacalenda took his temperature before sending for the doctor. The thermometer ran so high it broke,

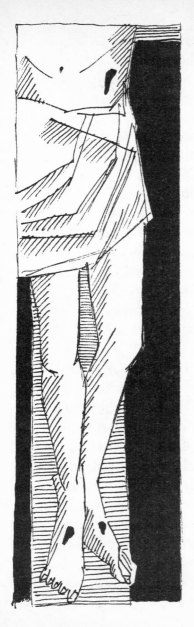

showing a reading of 108.5°F (42.5°C). Normal body temperature is 98.6° F (37°C), and anything above 105.8°F (41°C) is considered life-threatening. Father Paolina, knowing Padre Pio was a focus for strange phenomena, did not panic but got a larger thermometer and tried again. This time it showed 125.6°F (52°C). Nobody in a normal state could survive such heat, hot enough to cook an egg. Padre Pio said this was a spiritual fire burning in him. He said it caused a suffering he voluntarily endured to burn out the darkness and despair in the lives of people around him. Despite these fevers, he lived till he was eighty-one.

Many other strange and wonderful things happened to Padre Pio, giving people faith that life is more than just having a body. He renewed in people the belief that we have an eternal life, continuing even after our body dies. This was because people were healed of serious illnesses when Padre Pio prayed for them or touched them. He had the ability to make himself seen and to help people even when they were hundreds of miles away.

Being near Padre Pio changed the way people felt. By September 1955, so many people were visiting him that buildings at San Giovanni Rotundo had to be expanded to accommodate them. Thousands of letters arrived every month asking for his help.

Even with all this work, Padre Pio never left the friary. But it was obvious to those close to him that he was living not only within the normal time frame he shared with those around him, but also outside of time and space. Therefore, despite being at the friary constantly, some people met Padre Pio at distant places.

One person who had such a meeting was Cecil Humphrey-Smith, who was working for Heinz in Italy, checking tomato crops. Cecil had spent many sleepless nights worrying about the rain and hailstorms that were ruining the crops. One day, having driven a long way across bad roads, he fell asleep at the wheel and crashed into a bridge. His car broke in half and his injuries were severe. As he lay injured, he had a typical near-death experience of standing apart from his body, watching people carry his body to a car and on to the hospital.

At first Cecil was pronounced dead, and he watched his body being covered in a sheet and wheeled away. But another doctor found signs of life and revived him. As he lay close to death, a priest came in and sat next to him, telling him he must make confession so he could receive the last rites—the Catholic ritual performed for those about to die. The priest knew Cecil's entire life history, and got him to admit things about his life that he had kept hidden.

The next day another priest came. He and the staff told Cecil that nobody else had come to hear his confession.

Instantaneous Healing

Later, returning to England, Cecil developed a serious illness in which he experienced "brainstorms." At such times he lost control of his body, and the pain in his head was so severe that he smashed furniture, banged his head on walls, and suffered seizures. He was later found to have a growth in his brain.

A friend in Italy suggested he return there, and without telling him, took him to meet Padre Pio. Cecil immediately recognized the padre as the priest who had given him confession that night when he had been on the brink of death. Padre Pio reached out and tapped the left side of Cecil's head twice. Cecil's pain stopped immediately. X-rays later showed that the brain tumor was gone.

Cecil's symptoms never returned. He later learned that on the day of his car crash, the friend who had taken him to Padre Pio had prayed that his guardian angel ask Padre Pio for help.

How could Padre Pio be in two places at once? Some scientists believe that time is connected with speed. So if you were traveling at the speed of light—186,000 miles per second—you could be in many places at about the same time. The study of very small particles such as electrons shows that some things happen faster than the speed of light—instantaneously, in fact. If there is a part of our mind that also moves faster than light, we could experience things beyond what we usually know as time and space. You could be in many places at the same time. Time

wouldn't have the same meaning anymore.

Padre Pio taught that "Love is the first ingredient in the relief of suffering," and helping sick people, and praying to heal the sick in the world, were two of his main aims. In 1956, donations made by his followers were used to

build a hospital.

The padre's experiences had convinced him that when his body died he would move to an even better life. He promised people that when he moved to this bodiless, spiritual life, he would be even more powerful as a helper and healer than he was alive in the body. If thoughts and feelings are the means by which we reach those who are dead, thinking of Padre Pio and asking his help can still link you with him. Your feelings of love have the power to help those you want to help. Let your love shine.

Chapter Nine

Evelyn's Divining Adventures

As a child, instead of walking around clutching a doll, Evelyn Penrose wandered around with a dowsing rod in her hands. Her father had a remarkable ability to dowse and find water, so Evelyn had no doubts that divining worked. Evelyn was born in Cornwall on Midsummer Day at the turn of the century. Cornish people had an easy acceptance of old traditions like dowsing.

Holding a forked stick in the hands and using it to locate water, minerals, or objects is called divining or dowsing. The person who has this skill is called a dowser. Dowsing has a long history—divining rods are mentioned in the records of ancient Egypt and Rome.

Many dowsers claim that when they hold a dowsing rod and walk above an underground stream, the rod moves and twists independently. But in some cultures—in India, for example—dowsers did not use rods or pendulums. Instead they became aware of the water through spontaneous movements or sensations in their own bodies. So it is most likely that the divining rod is moved by unconscious sensitivity acting on the body, which makes the rod move. If the rod were really moving on its own, a rod attached to the front of a stroller, for example, would move when it went over an underground stream. It doesn't.

Finding Minerals with a Twig

Living in Cornwall as a child, Evelyn knew that dowsing had been used to discover some of the local tin mines. Many times she also saw her father successfully find water for people. So it wasn't strange that she too became a professional dowser when she grew up.

Although Evelyn used the rod or pendulum when dowsing, she experienced powerful physical reactions to different minerals. Often she felt things emotionally as well. All this suggests that her skill was another example of the mind's ability to extend awareness beyond the body and the limitations of our five senses.

Evelyn never went to a school of dowsing. In some cultures—in parts of Africa, for example—dowsers are given long training. In his book *Lightning Bird*, Lyall Watson describes how in African tribal life students are trained to develop their intuition. Part of their training is to find lost objects, and they must practice and practice until their success rate is very high and they are acutely aware of the process. Some of the methods they use are to allow spontaneous body movements and to develop the ability to let the mind and emotions express themselves without attempting to control them. In this way the conscious mind is bypassed and unconscious intuitions can make themselves known.

Evelyn's only training was watching and working with her father, and then having her abilities tested.

While she was in California, for instance, she wanted to see if she could locate underground oil in the oil fields. She was taken around four sites without being told in advance whether their oil yield was good or not. Evelyn said, "The reaction was far more powerful than any I had obtained from water, or even from tin or copper." Because her reactions were so strong—strong enough to make her feel ill—she was able to tell which well was producing the most oil.

The deputy manager who was showing her around the site then took her to a well that he suggested was producing. When Evelyn tested it, though, she got no reaction. The deputy manager then told her it was actually a dry well. He had let her work on it to test her ability. But Evelyn found that dowsing for oil was very stressful, and would sometimes faint while working.

Paid to Be Intuitive

Evelyn was asked to work for the Canadian government. No rain had fallen for years in British Columbia, and the many apple orchards in the province were dying. So the Department of Agriculture employed Evelyn as their official water diviner.

Her first task was to look for water in a wonderful orchard in a place called Okanagan Valley. "It was a great shock to see this orchard," she said, "covering the side of a large hill, wilting and dying, and to hear the owner say quite simply that he was facing disaster. We stopped and looked up the hill and he was telling me something when, suddenly, I was nearly thrown off my feet.

I grabbed his arm to steady myself. 'Water,' I gasped. 'Water! Lots and lots of water.' I can never stand over underground water without being swung about, and the greater the amount of water the greater the reaction."

A well was dug over the site Evelyn marked, and it hit water at six feet. At twelve feet the well was easily producing 108,000 gallons a day. The orchard was saved. The locals called it the Wonder Well. Evelyn went on to discover wells all over the British Columbian countryside.

Later in her life Evelyn found she could dowse a site without going there. She could get equally good results working on a map. Today many dowsers can work this way.

Body Dowsing

Dowsing could be defined as a way of letting the body tell us what it knows. In other words, we stop our head from working overtime and give our body space to say something in its own way—namely, through movement and mime. So to learn how to dowse we must first learn how to let the body "speak," or express itself. An interesting and fun way to begin is to use the arm-on-the-wall test. Here is how you do it.

The Magic Arm Test

We need to be a bit playful to get the best out of this, so let's start by giving our body a few minutes of free space. See if you can let some yawns happen, for example. Close your eyes, relax, and slowly act out the movements of a yawn—slowly open your mouth really wide, and . . . y-a-w-n. If you're doing it right, as you start acting the movement, the yawn will take over and become a spontaneous movement all by itself. When that happens, try it a few more times to get the feel of letting your body make its own movements.

Now for the arm test. Stand about a foot away from a wall, with your right side to the wall and your right hand next to a clear space on the wall.

Keeping your arm straight, lift your right arm side-

ways until the back of your hand is against the wall.
Because you are next to the wall and your arm is

1 ft

straight, you will only manage to lift your arm part of
the way. So when the back of your hand touches
the wall, press it hard against the wall, as if you were
trying to complete the movement of lifting the arm.
Don't lean on the wall—just keep your arm straight
and try as hard as you can to complete the lifting
motion.

Using a reasonable amount of effort, hold that
position—with your hand pressing against the wall—
for about twenty seconds. Then move so that you're
facing away from the wall. Keep your eyes closed

and stay relaxed—and just be aware of what happens.

Try the experiment before reading on, and then repeat it with the left arm. In fact, try it a couple of times with each arm before you read the next paragraph.

If you have learned—from the yawning exercise—how to let your body do its own thing, then your arm will have moved upward by itself. If it was a strong reaction, your arm will have floated right up with a wonderful feeling. If you consciously moved your own arm, then it wasn't working.

Whatever happened, try it again with each arm. Practice will improve your ability to just let go.

A Simple Dowsing Kit

To make a simple dowsing kit you need a fairly strong wire coat hanger and two small empty bottles about four or five inches high. The bottles should be small enough around so you can hold one in each hand.

Cut the coat hanger into two L-shapes. The longest side of the L should be able to sit in the bottle neck and be about an inch longer than the depth of the bottle. It should then be able to move or swing easily on the point in the bottle.

Put one L-shape in each bottle, with the longest side in the neck. Hold one bottle in each hand, and at first tilt the bottle slightly forward so the shorter arm of the L swings forward. Then level up, and you are ready to begin using your dowsing kit.

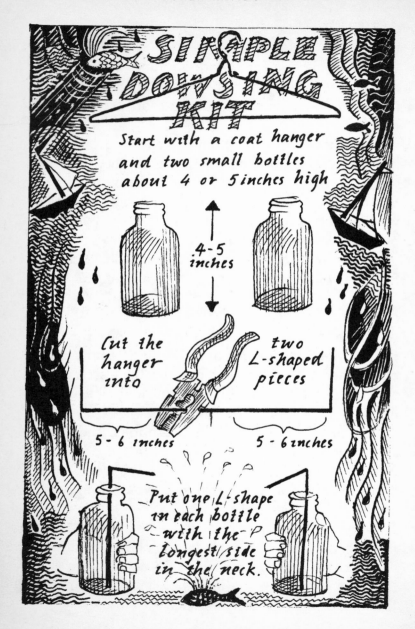

SIMPLE DOWSING KIT

Start with a coat hanger and two small bottles about 4 or 5 inches high

4 - 5 inches

Cut the hanger into

two L-shaped pieces

5 - 6 inches

5 - 6 inches

Put one L-shape in each bottle with the longest side in the neck.

Learning to Dowse

Dowsing works because your conscious and unconscious minds make an agreement about certain aims and signals. This is like agreeing with a friend that a certain signal between the two of you will mean "start," and another will mean "stop."

Here is a sample aim and some simple signals. Work on these, and you may find yourself starting to develop some skill at dowsing.

AIM: To let my body express itself without interfering too much. In this way I am trying to let my unconscious knowledge or intuition become known to me consciously.

SIGNALS: When the wire L rods point straight ahead, that is neutral. When the rods point inward toward each other, that represents a "yes" signal. When the wire rods point outward away from each other, that is a "no" signal.

To start your training, you can try the "finding game" African trainees use. Have a friend hide an object without telling you where they put it—it can be indoors or outdoors. Then, holding the bottles, walk around and watch the signals given by the swinging arms of the L rods. As you get nearer the object, the rods should swing toward each other more and more. If you move further away, the rods should swing apart.

Obviously you will need to test your own intuition and practice often to get beyond the stage where you are consciously influencing the rods. At the next stage, your feelings and desires influence the rods. If you relax these too, then your intuition can flow through.

Once you begin to be able to find hidden objects, you can start looking for water.

Chapter Ten

Animal Children

Rudyard Kipling's *Jungle Book* stories about Mowgli, the boy who was lost in the jungle as a baby and raised by wolves, were fiction, but they were based on fact. Throughout history, and in all parts of the world, children have been discovered who were raised by animals. According to legend, Romulus and his twin brother Remus, who are said to have founded Rome in about 700 B.C., were suckled by a she-wolf and discovered by a shepherd.

Babies raised by animals did not only happen in the past. On April 17, 1991, around the time the film *Dances with Wolves* was popular, the following headline appeared in the British newspaper the *Daily Star:* "TRAGIC BOY'S DANCE IN WOLF'S LAIR." The story goes on to say: "A tragic orphan brought up by a pack of wild wolves will never be able to live like a normal man, say doctors. The boy who REALLY danced with the wolves was aged about seven when he was found 29 years ago in the wastes of southern Russia by a team of oil explorers. He howled like a wolf and savagely bit one of the oilmen, who christened him Djuma—the Wolf Boy.

"Professor Rufat Kazirbayev said doctors had battled to reeducate him to act like

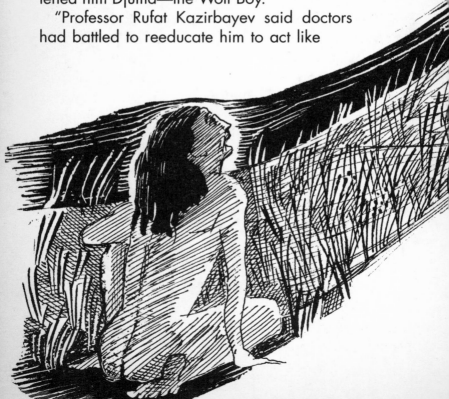

a normal human being, but failed. They are now giving up the fight. Professor Kazirbayev said that 'His mind is with the wolves. He will howl at the moon for the rest of his life.'"

At the age of thirty-seven, Djuma was still in the hospital. He still crawled on all fours, ate raw meat, and bit people when he was frightened. He could speak only in disjointed phrases, such as "Mother dead. Father dead. Brother dead. Sister dead. Mother nice. Father bad."

Dr. Anna Ticheenskaya, one of the doctors who looked after Djuma, said, "Presumably his family were killed in a political purge. He has shown us in sign language how, when his mother was killed, she saved him by throwing herself over his body."

The Man Who Is A Wolf

Djuma has learned to brush his hair and his teeth and use the toilet, "like a trained animal." But when taken to the zoo he howls, as if he is begging the animals to take him to freedom. Sadly, that will never happen. Djuma will probably spend the rest of his life in the clinic, where, doctors say, he spends his days like a dog—half asleep and dreaming.

What Djuma's life teaches us is that being human, being aware of oneself as a unique person, isn't something that just happens by itself as we grow. Djuma is a wolf, even though he has what we think is a human body and brain. Some of the things people like Djuma lack that you and I take for granted are a sense of time—that is, an awareness of a past and future—and a sense of identity, a certainty that we are a person with a name. This sense of identity leads us to say things like, "I am Sam" or "I am Sarah." When we have a sense of "I am," we also have feelings such as guilt, confidence, shyness, and we feel separate from other people and animals.

Children brought up by animals, unless they are recovered when they are very young, do not have a sense of time. They lack any feeling of personal identity, and they feel connected only with other animals and nature. You might say they are like Adam or Eve, feeling at one with nature.

At seven, it was too late for Djuma to develop into a human. The special thing he lacked was other humans talking to him so that he could learn speech. Language may be something like a piece of computer software our brain uses to understand time and separateness, and to form a sense of identity—usually around the name we have been given. This is no doubt why baptism and other social naming ceremonies are so important in so many cultures.

The Animal Boy of Aveyron

Victor, who was named the Wild Boy of Aveyron, was discovered in the French countryside in 1800. Some villagers from Aveyron, in the south of France, captured a boy of about eleven or twelve who had been running wild and naked, even though it was winter. His body was marked with scars where he had been scratched and injured in fights with animals. Although the villagers tried to speak with Victor, he didn't seem to pay attention, and it soon became apparent that he didn't know any language. At first people thought he was deaf and mute. All he was interested in was trying to escape.

The story of Victor's capture spread quickly, and he was taken to Paris to be studied. At that time there was a popular belief that the "natural" human being was superior to the civilized person. This was called the idea of the "Noble Savage." However, to the inhabitants of Paris, Victor showed no signs of nobility.

He was described as "a disgusting, slovenly boy, affected with spasmodic . . . convulsive motions . . . biting and scratching those who contradicted him, expressing no kind of affection for those who attended upon him." He was therefore thought to be an idiot and was imprisoned in a home for deaf-mutes.

Fortunately, a young doctor named Jean-Marc Itard looked after the "wild boy" and tried to educate him. It was Dr. Itard who gave him the name Victor.

At first Victor learned quickly. Dr. Itard realized, from watching Victor, that he was not deaf, mute, or stupid. He was a normal, healthy boy, but he had never been taught how to do the things most of us take for granted, like sitting in a chair, using the toilet, and not biting people when he met them. Within a few months Victor could sit in a chair, express his emotions without being violent, and he could even speak

a few words, like "milk" and "Oh God," which was something Dr. Itard's housekeeper, Madame Guerin, often said. Victor also came to like Madame Guerin, who fed and cared for him.

After a few months, Victor's progress slowed down to the point where he stopped learning new words. In his years with whatever animals had raised him, Victor had missed some vital stage of mental growth that would have given him the ability to learn continuously and easily. He never made up for that loss. Like Djuma the wolf boy, he had missed the years when language and relationships with other people "taught" him to recognize his own identity, and programed him to learn and even come up with new ideas and discoveries. Instead of imitating other human beings, he had learned to imitate his animal parents. His imitation was too complete.

Victor stayed in Paris with Madame Guerin until the age of forty, when he died.

You Could Be a Wolf, a Human, or a Star

Many other children, girls as well as boys, have been recovered from the wild. In 1920, two girls were found in Midnapore, India. They were given the names Amala and Kamala. Like Djuma and Victor, they never learned to speak, and became trained but trapped animals. They died fairly young, unable to adapt to their life with humans.

The stories of these children's lives show us the enormous influence the early years of learning have on our mind. If in early childhood we can learn to be a wolf, a bear, or a human, why don't we recognize this and teach babies to be more than human? Perhaps such training would be a step toward reducing the murder, aggression, and mental poverty that are so widespread in the world today.

It also leads one to wonder what happened in human evolution to produce speech, and whether animal-like humans like Djuma and Victor ever existed alongside fully linguistic humans. If so, did they communicate with one another?

Some Other Animal or Isolated Children

Leopard child of India—discovered in 1920
Wolf child of Jhansi, India—discovered in 1933
Confined child of Ohio—discovered in 1938
Gazelle child of Syria—discovered in 1946
Ape child of Teheran—discovered in 1961
Genie, confined child of Los Angeles—discovered in 1970
Interesting Internet site—
http://www.plu.edu/~jensenmk/271 wild.html

What's It Like to Be an Animal?

Animals do not think in words as we do. Therefore they don't speak to themselves or each other in the same way we do. But they do feel and respond to things. So if you want to see what it's like to be an animal, stop thinking about things and instead be aware of what you feel. Without thinking about whether it's right or wrong, without asking anyone's opinion, tune in to what your feelings want you to do.

Maybe you want to hide under the table, the way some dogs do. Or maybe you want to sit on someone's lap, like a cat. For a while, can you dare to do that? If you let everyone know that just for a while you're being a cat or a dog, it will probably be fine.

Chapter Eleven

Helen Keller—The Sighted Blind

Until she was nineteen months old, Helen Keller was a normal, happy baby living with loving parents. She had just started to talk, and had learned one word when she was playing outside in the yard. It had started to rain and, loving the feeling of the raindrops, she learned the word *water*.

Very soon after that, Helen contracted scarlet fever. The illness was severe, and it left her blind and deaf.

Helen was born in 1880, and at that time there were no schools for the blind and deaf as there are now. She was therefore left to grow and learn as best she could. But being blind and deaf, she was as cut off from being able to learn from the people around her as the children reared by animals were. Like them, she grew wild and violent, and had no sense of her own existence.

Then, when she was six years old, Helen's parents arranged for Anne Sullivan, a teacher of the deaf and dumb, to come and try to help their daughter. Anne taught by touching her fingers to Helen's hand, and spelling out words through movements. She would, for instance, put an apple in Helen's hand, then spell *apple* with her fingers. It was very difficult. Helen could not make the leap connecting Anne's finger movements with the object she held in her hand. It seemed as if Helen was trapped forever in her dark, silent world.

The Leap Beyond Darkness

Then one day there was a wonderful breakthrough. Anne had put one of Helen's hands into water running from an outdoor pump. She spelled out the word water with finger movements, and Helen suddenly made the extraordinary leap that we all make at some time—from knowing nothing but feelings to being able to think and communicate. Describing that moment, Helen said, "Suddenly I felt . . . a thrill of returning thought; and somehow the mystery of language was revealed to me."

Because most us were much younger when the wonder of language and thought flowered in us, we may not remember such an amazing moment. But for Helen, waking up to what we take for granted came when she was old enough to appreciate it.

Trying to explain what it was like to live without words and thought, Helen said that although she existed, she didn't *know* she existed. There was no

pain, because there was no "Helen" to feel any pain, only a body with sensations. She existed as a sort of nothingness. When she remembered that one word, *water,* she said that the "nothingness was blotted out." If she had never learned that one word before becoming blind and deaf, she might have remained in her nothingness forever.

From the moment when Helen felt the water on her hand, woke up to being a person, and opened the door to being able to speak, it seemed that she could see with her fingertips. Seeing with her fingers was not at all dull for her. "Sometimes it seems as if the very substance of my flesh were so many eyes looking out," she said. "I only know that the world I see

with my fingers is alive, ruddy, and satisfying."

The World at Her Fingertips

The excitement of being a person didn't leave Helen. She wanted to know all about the world, and explore it with the sight, hearing, and sensitivity of her "seeing" fingers. Not only could she see with her fingers, she could also feel people's emotions through them. She said, "Occasionally, if I am very fortunate, I place my hand gently on a small tree and feel the happy quiver of a bird in full song." With her fingers she could "detect laughter, sorrow, and many other obvious emotions. I know my friends from the feel of their faces."

Helen became famous throughout the world, wrote several books including *The Story of My Life*, and lectured to people about being blind and the wonders we can all "see" in one way or another. Through her lectures and her books she raised money to help the handicapped. Helen's life and work prompted the development of many new techniques for helping the blind and deaf.

People who met Helen often said that she appeared to be aware of things they had no sense of. She could feel a person's presence, and perhaps because her senses other than sight and hearing were so acutely developed, she was much more aware of what was going on around her than most people with normal vision and hearing could be.

From an Animal I Grew to Be ME!

Unlike the animal children mentioned in the previous chapter, Helen was able to emerge into what we know as ordinary human life. What happened to Helen shows very clearly the importance of learning how to speak, or being able to communicate one's thoughts and desires to other people.

Helen's life and the lives of the animal children suggest that in a real sense, our personal existence is actually given to us by people around us when we are a baby. The people who teach us to speak help us understand who and what we are.

In looking back on her years before she knew herself as Helen, she says that it was like existing in a dream. She had only physical sensations, which passed quickly. Without any personal center or name around which impressions could form like a crystal, her sensations had no lasting influence on her.

Helen Keller died in 1968.

What Is It Like to Be Blind and Dumb?

When I was eighteen I had an eye injury and had to lie in a hospital bed for six weeks with both eyes bandaged. It was an extraordinary and wonderful experience. I responded to people in a very different way from when I could see them. Because I wasn't confused by how people looked, I had a much clearer feeling about what sort of person I was meeting.

If you have the support of those around you, it is well worth being "blind" for a day by keeping your eyes covered. See if you can learn to move, eat, meet people, and go about your ordinary daily tasks without the help of your sight.

If you try it, you will almost certainly discover a new world and discover many things about yourself.

Chapter Twelve

George Washington Carver— From Slave to Genius

In 1860 a baby boy was born to a black slave woman living on a plantation in Missouri. The child was weak, and while he was still tiny, slave raiders attacked the farm and kidnapped the mother and child to sell further south. Moses Carver, the owner of the plantation, pursued the raiders all the way to Arkansas. He found the baby abandoned, but never caught up with the raiders to retrieve the mother.

The baby was allowed to live in Moses Carver's

house. He stayed frail, so when he was old enough to work he was only expected to do light housework. For some time the boy had no name, but because of his characteristic of telling the truth, Moses Carver called him George Washington, and gave him the family name Carver.

George was allowed to spend many hours each day doing whatever he liked. He taught himself to cook and care for the house. He often wandered in the woods, watching the animals and fascinated by the plants and trees. Without anyone teaching him, he started sketching the plant life of the countryside. He also had a secret garden in the woods, where he collected and cultivated many unusual plants.

George had a deep insight into plants, and he became known as the "plant doctor" because of his ability to heal diseased plants and rid them of pests. His reputation spread, and people a long way off sent him sick plants to cure.

Through his own study and devotion, George not only developed these talents but also became a fine painter and musician.

A Longing to Learn

The Carvers acknowledged George's need to learn, but they had no money to spare for his education. So George found an old spelling book and taught himself to read and write. He spent hours studying by himself, until at ten he discovered an old log-cabin schoolhouse in a nearby town.

Working at small jobs, he managed to earn

enough money to pay for his schooling. But the school was too far to walk to, so George slept wherever he could find a sheltered spot. At the end of a year he had learned all the teacher could offer.

Still hungry for knowledge, George moved to Fort Scott in Kansas and attended high school there. To pay for his food and lodging, he washed dishes, cooked, laundered people's clothes, worked at anything he could for seven years. That was how long it took to get his high school diploma.

Still not satisfied after his high school graduation, George wondered where to go next. All the colleges in the South were closed to black people. He applied to a northern college, but having saved his fare and traveled to the university, was again disappointed to find that they also refused "coloreds." Eventually he was accepted at Simpson College, and in 1894 received his bachelor of science degree from Iowa State College in Ames. He received his master's degree two years later.

The Man Who Talks with Flowers

For a while George taught botany at Iowa State, where he was also in charge of the bacteriological laboratory and greenhouse, but his lifework was still awaiting him. This began with a call back south in 1897, to the Tuskegee Institute in Alabama. It was here, with little salary, no equipment, and in barren surroundings, that he became known as a saint and scientist—the "man who talks with flowers."

At that time the American South was a devastated place. For years the farmers had continually planted cotton. Now, with boll weevils attacking their crops, impoverished soil, and despondent spirits, many farmers were trying to support their families on about $300 a year.

Seeing these conditions as his train carried him south, Dr. Carver felt a rush of purpose. Here was the work his whole life had been leading to—the regeneration of the South that had rejected him.

Something else was at work inside him, too. In the preceding years, as his inner strength had carried him through the difficulties of education, something had opened within him. He had learned how to pray.

To reeducate the farmers, many of whom were black, George would load a mule-drawn cart with seeds and plants, and travel around the South teaching and lecturing. He gave much more than agricultural information. Preaching crop rotation, and the planting of sweet potatoes and peanuts to enrich the soil, he gradually led the way not only to rich fields and crops again, but also to new spiritual harvests.

Spiritual Teacher, Earthly Agriculturist

Jim Hardwick, talking about one of George's lectures, said, "One day he came to the town where I lived and gave an address on his discoveries of the peanut. I went to the lecture expecting to learn about science and came away knowing more about prayer than I had ever learned in the theological schools.

And to cap the climax, when the old gentleman was leaving the hall he turned to me, where I stood transfixed and inspired, and said, 'I want you to be one of my boys!'"

But Jim Hardwick was white, born into a southern family that had once owned black slaves. It was very difficult for Jim to imagine being part of a black man's "family"—even his spiritual family. It took Jim several days of wrestling with this ingrained pride before he could overcome this barrier and feel ready to share the inner life of Dr. Carver. When that finally happened, he says, "Instantly it seemed that his spirit filled that room. . . . A peace entered me, and my problems fell away."

The results of George's work with southern farmers grew beyond anything he had expected. Farm after farm used his methods. The soil changed, and crop production increased, until one year the harvest of peanuts and sweet potatoes was so big the market couldn't absorb them. People couldn't sell their crops.

Shocked that his work had had such an outcome, and seeing the threat of a disaster, George didn't ask for government aid, or demand that people stop planting. He went into his laboratory to pray. In his own words, "I went into my laboratory and said, 'Dear Mr. Creator, please tell me what the universe was made for?' The Creator answered, 'You want to know too much for that little mind of yours. Ask for something more your size.'

"Then I asked, 'Dear Mr. Creator, tell me what man was made for?' Again the great Creator replied,

'Little man, you are still asking too much. Cut down the extent of your request, and improve the intent.'

"So then I asked, 'Please, Mr. Creator, will you tell me why the peanut was made?'

"'That's better, but even then it's infinite. What do you want to know about the peanut?'

"'Mr. Creator, can I make milk out of the peanut?'"

Power of Prayer in the Laboratory

George locked himself in his laboratory for several days and nights listening to his intuition and analyzing the peanut. When he emerged, he said God and he had solved the problem. From the peanut, and later the pecan and the sweet potato, George Washington Carver discovered how to extract, or synthesize, face powders, printer's ink, peanut butter, shampoo, creosote, vinegar, dandruff remedy, dyes, synthetic rubber compound, soaps, wood stains, and hundreds of other products. "The great Creator gave us three kingdoms, the animal, vegetable, and mineral," said George. "Now he has added a fourth, the synthetic kingdom."

George said the secret of his incredible inventive genius came from love. "When I touch a flower, I am not merely touching that flower, I am touching infinity." He went on to say, "Anything will give up its secrets if you love it enough. Not only have I found that when I talk to the little flower or to the peanut they will give up their secrets, but I have found that when I silently commune with people, they give up their secrets also if you love them enough."

Chapter Thirteen

I Died—But I'm Alive

When young Debbie N. lay dying in the hospital, she suddenly started saying to the nurses that her brother had come to meet her, and was telling her not to be afraid of death. The strange thing was that Debbie had never been told she had a brother who had died. Her parents were amazed when they heard what Debbie had said. They had kept their son's death a secret.

Debbie had looked through the door of death as it opened to receive her. But some people pass through the door and come back to tell us what it was like.

Sam was a baby when his mother died.[2] When he was only four, something weird and wonderful happened to him. He was playing with some boys at a millstream. Just as the mill gates opened, one of his friends pushed him into deeper water. Sam was dragged under by the flood and drowned. A few

[2] I have given fictitious names to Debbie and Sam, but they are real people.

boys ran for help, but by the time Sam was pulled out, he was apparently dead.

Visiting the World of the Dead

After tense minutes of resuscitation, Sam breathed again. As his father carried him home, Sam excitedly told him that something amazing had happened in the water. Sam said he felt himself being dragged down into the water. Everything went black, and he seemed to sink further and further. Then he felt a change and experienced a rising feeling, as if he were floating upward. Gradually it got lighter, and he surfaced above the water in the waves of a great sea. Other people were surfacing too, and they were all carried toward the shore, where people were waiting for them.

As Sam got near the beach he saw his grandmother and grandfather waving to him. In front of them stood his mother, so pleased to see him. She bent down to lift him out of the water, catching hold of his arms. As she did so, a cross she was wearing around her neck swung down in front of Sam's face, and sparkling on the cross Sam saw seven jewels.

Just at that moment Sam felt himself dragged back, down into the darkness again. When he came out of the darkness he was on the riverbank, in his father's arms.

As Sam told this story, his father said nothing. It was only years later that he told Sam something he had kept as a precious secret. Sam's mother had died suddenly, on her birthday. Before this Sam's father

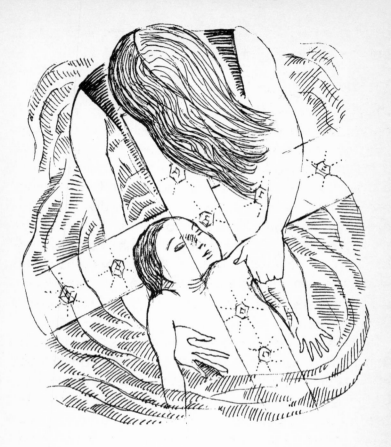

had bought a special birthday present to surprise her with—a cross with seven jewels on it. After she died, but before she was buried, Sam's father, telling nobody, opened his wife's coffin and lovingly placed the cross around her neck. So when Sam had told him about the cross, he was so overcome with emotion that he hadn't been able to say anything to his son.

Leaving the Body Behind

Many children and adults have what is called a "near-death-experience," or NDE. This may occur when they are ill, or because of an accident. For instance, eleven-year-old Brad Steiger was caught in the blades of a large piece of machinery on his parents' farm in Iowa. He suffered several skull fractures as the metal blades hit his head. While he was in the borderline state between life and death, Brad felt himself drift away from his body and was able to watch what was happening from a distance. He could see his injured body on the ground, and he saw his sister run for help. He watched his father carrying him, and at the same time felt some of the sensations of being in his father's arms. While he was out of his body he also became aware of knowledge far beyond anything he'd ever known before—he was able to see the patterns and processes of life. Although he was very young, he felt he had been shown a plan of the universe and how people's lives fit into it. He wanted to tell people that we are all part of eternal life, and are not alone in the universe.

When people experience being out of their body they are able to do and know things they are not usually capable of. When I was eighteen and living in Germany, I had such an experience, and was able to see what my mother was doing in London. But a truly fascinating example of this appeared in the *Scotsman* newspaper of February 27, 1937, in a story about a talk given at the Royal Medical Society in Edinburgh.

In this talk, Sir Aukland Geddes described the case of a doctor friend who, late one night, suddenly became ill with acute gastroenteritis. At ten o'clock the man had tried to telephone for help, but found himself unable to move. Gradually he felt as if he were being split in two. One part was outside, separate from his body, while the other remained in his body. The awareness outside his body grew stronger, and the body consciousness disappeared. He was dying from his illness, and could watch his body from a distance.

Then the man began to realize that he could see not only his body, but any other person he concentrated

on, no matter where in the world they were. He could instantly be with whoever he thought about, see what they were doing, and even know what they were thinking.

Someone came into the room where the man's sick body was dying. He observed that person running to the telephone to call a doctor, and the doctor answering on the distant telephone. As he watched his own body and the bodies of the other people, it seemed to him that the brain was like a receiver of impressions not just from the three-dimensional world where our body exists, but also from dimensions beyond that. So the mind was not in the brain, but the brain was in the midst of the mind, like a radio is within radio signals.

The Brain Is a Radio Set in an Ocean of Mind

Near-death experiences suggest that our awareness can sometimes reach far beyond the limitations of our sight, hearing, and touch. We live in a universe in which our mind is still a largely unknown territory. Scientifically we have traveled further within our solar system than within the huge space of the human mind.

Perhaps you will be one of those lucky enough to know the adventure and wonder of helping chart those infinite spaces of the mind.